World of Paper Snowflakes

Learn to fold and cut with 26 unique design templates

ROY YAP

ISBN-10:069299145X
ISBN-13: 978-0-692-99145

CONTENTS

ACKNOWLEDGMENTS

I would like to express my deepest gratitude to Reema and Juliet who put in the time and effort in helping to edit this book.

To my friends and family who have been so supportive and encouraged me to take the step in sharing my artistic design with the world.

Last but not least, thank you to NASA for the generous selection of free photos like the "Space Station Flyover of the Mediterranean" seen on the cover.

INTRODUCTION

I began designing and cutting out paper snowflakes in December 2012, after hearing about the mass shooting at Sandy Hook Elementary. Several Parent Teacher Student Associations wanted to create a Winter Wonderland at the school to welcome students back, and they put out a national request for paper snowflakes. Feeling inspired to try creating my own snowflake, I joined co-workers in our company's effort to contribute snowflakes. I have been cutting and designing snowflakes ever since.

My enthusiasm and joy for snowflake cutting had me designing all year round. Currently, I have about 153 unique designs - everything from early experimentation to my unique templates, much of which are inspired just from my creative juices. Friends and family are always fascinated by my intricate designs, and my stunning and surprising paper snowflake reveals.

With urging and encouragement from my friends and family to put together a book, I created <u>World of Paper Snowflakes</u> and am excited to share my designs with you. I hope that you enjoy using these templates to fold and cut snowflakes, and go even further to experiment with creating your very own designs.

In this book, you will find an introduction to the very basics of making paper snowflakes. I have also arranged the designs from easy to advanced in the hopes that it will give you hours of joy, learning, and experimenting. Also included are web links where you will find more information, including links to instructional videos that will further enhance the step by step process.

A little interesting snowflake factoid: real snowflakes are only 6 sided. When the molecules in the ice crystals bond together, they do so in a hexagonal shape, forming a six-sided flake. For fun, I wanted to defy this design; and, in this book, I have included four and eight-sided snowflake designs, since they have more room and spires to play and design with.

I hope you enjoy using these paper snowflake templates. Please feel free to reach out to me with any comments, feedback, suggestions or requests using the contact details at the end of the book.

RECOMMENDED TOOLS AND MATERIALS

The most fundamental tools and materials that you will need are a comfortable pair of sharp scissors and paper.

For more detailed work, these tools are optional, but also very helpful to have:
- Small, sharp detail scissors (for detailed and minute cuts. Example: Judkins CTS11 retails for about $8)
- General 7 in. - 7.5 in. scissors (example: Scotch/Craft Smart)
- Tonic Studios Tim Holtz 817 Kushgrip Non Stick Micro Serrated Snips, 7 in. (around $10)
- Craft knife (example: x-acto #1 around $4)
- ¼ in. / regular single hole punch
- Paper choices:
  - Regular white printing paper
  - Origami paper (already in a square shape, thin / lightweight)
  - Wrapping paper (creates an extra layer of festive design and color)
  - Coffee filters
  - Used printed paper, used square Post-IT notes (good way to recycle and get interesting patterns)
  - Construction Paper is not ideal because it is thicker so it becomes more difficult to fold and cut
- Cutting board (paired with craft knife to prevent damage to table surface)
- Paper / recycle bin to catch paper bits

BASICS OF FOLDING AND PREPARING A 6-SIDED SNOWFLAKE

1. Take a regular 8.5" x 11" copy paper, in portrait layout, and fold the top left to the bottom right into a triangle to form a perfect square. Cut the bottom off. **NOTE:** For origami paper just perform the fold as it is already a square paper.

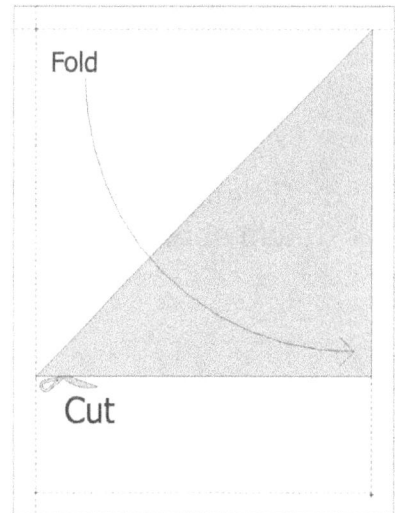

Fold

Cut

2. Take the bottom left and fold to the top right to make a ½ triangle.

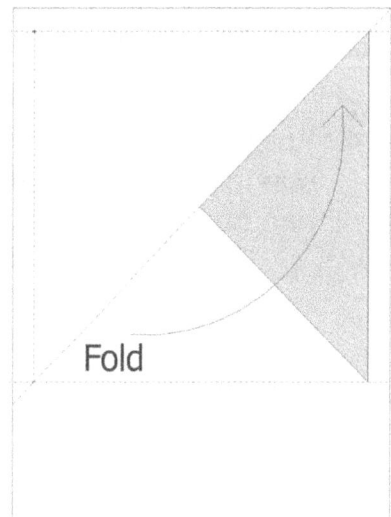

Fold

3. Rotate counter clockwise (to the left) and then fold about ⅓ from the right tip to the left.

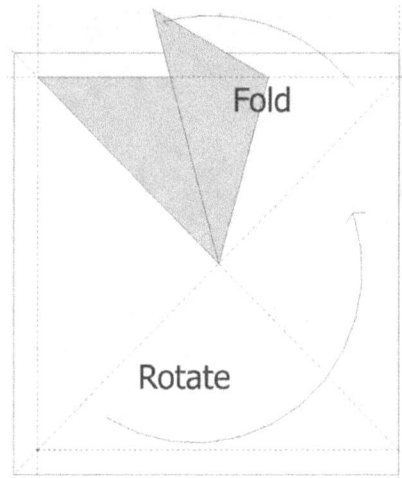

4. Fold from the left tip to the right. **NOTE:** You can fold both the tips on top of each other or one on each side making a zig zag "Z" shape

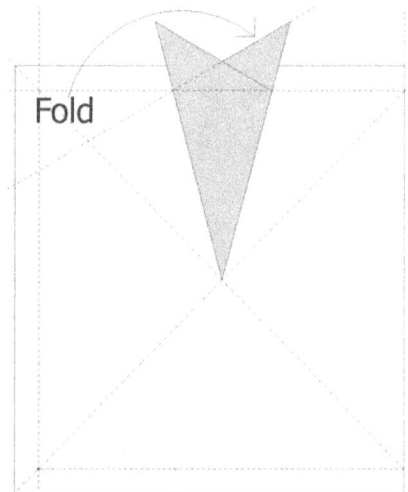

5. Cut the top tails off and you're ready to copy the template to your 6-sided paper snowflake

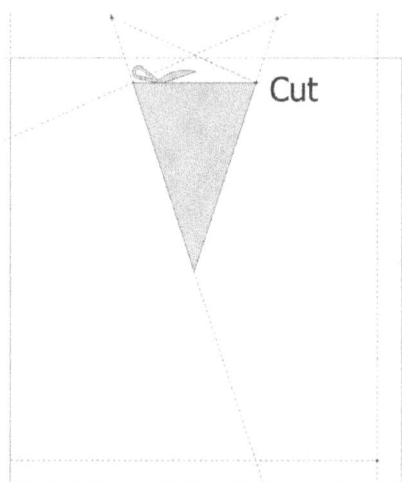

BASICS OF FOLDING AND PREPARING AN 8-SIDED SNOWFLAKE

1. Take a regular 8.5" x 11" copy paper, in portrait layout and fold the top left to the bottom right, into a triangle to form a perfect square. Cut the bottom off. **NOTE**: For origami paper just perform the fold as it is already a square paper.

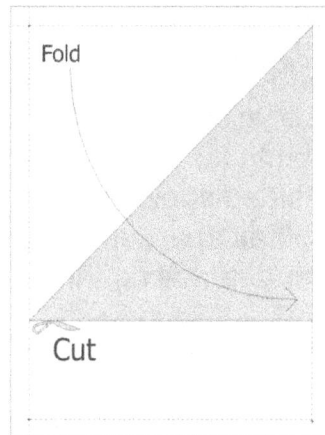

2. Open up the triangle back to the perfect square shape. Fold the square paper in half by taking the bottom and fold to the top.

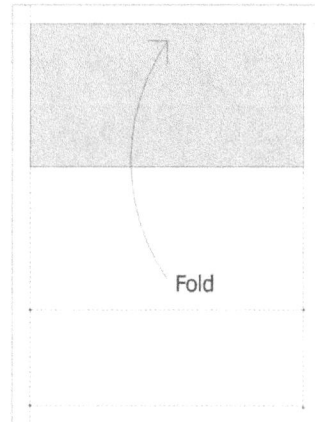

3. Fold the paper in half again by taking the left to the right.

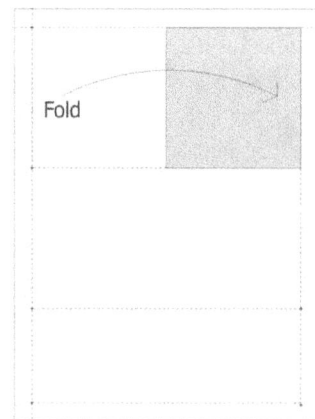

4. Fold the paper in half again by taking the top left and folding it to the bottom right. **NOTE:** This is an important fold to follow to ensure that 8 sided snowflake will connect and not fall apart after the cutting is done and revealing the pattern.

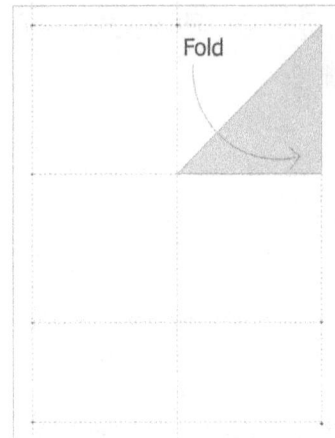

Fold

GUIDES, TIPS, AND TRICKS TO USING SNOWFLAKE TEMPLATES

Each of the templates have folding guide lines (dotted lines). Each page has a solid / darker colored area which represents the areas to be cut out after you have folded them. There is also a preview of the finished product at the bottom right of each page to help guide you.

You can cut out straight from the book, trace the template to your favorite paper, or photocopy. You can also resize photocopied designs and fit multiples on one page. I would highly recommend using a standard ¼ inch hole punch for circular cuts. You could try using scissors to make a discreet cut from the folded area to connect to the circular cut, and from there, finish the circular cut. You can also use a craft knife to cut the circular holes or to poke the folded paper as a starting position to insert your scissors.

Many of the more advanced snowflake templates can actually be achieved by scissors alone. For smaller lines and harder to reach areas, it may be easier to cut from the outside in towards your outline, and discard extra paper in your way.

ACORN DIAMOND

SNOW ANGEL

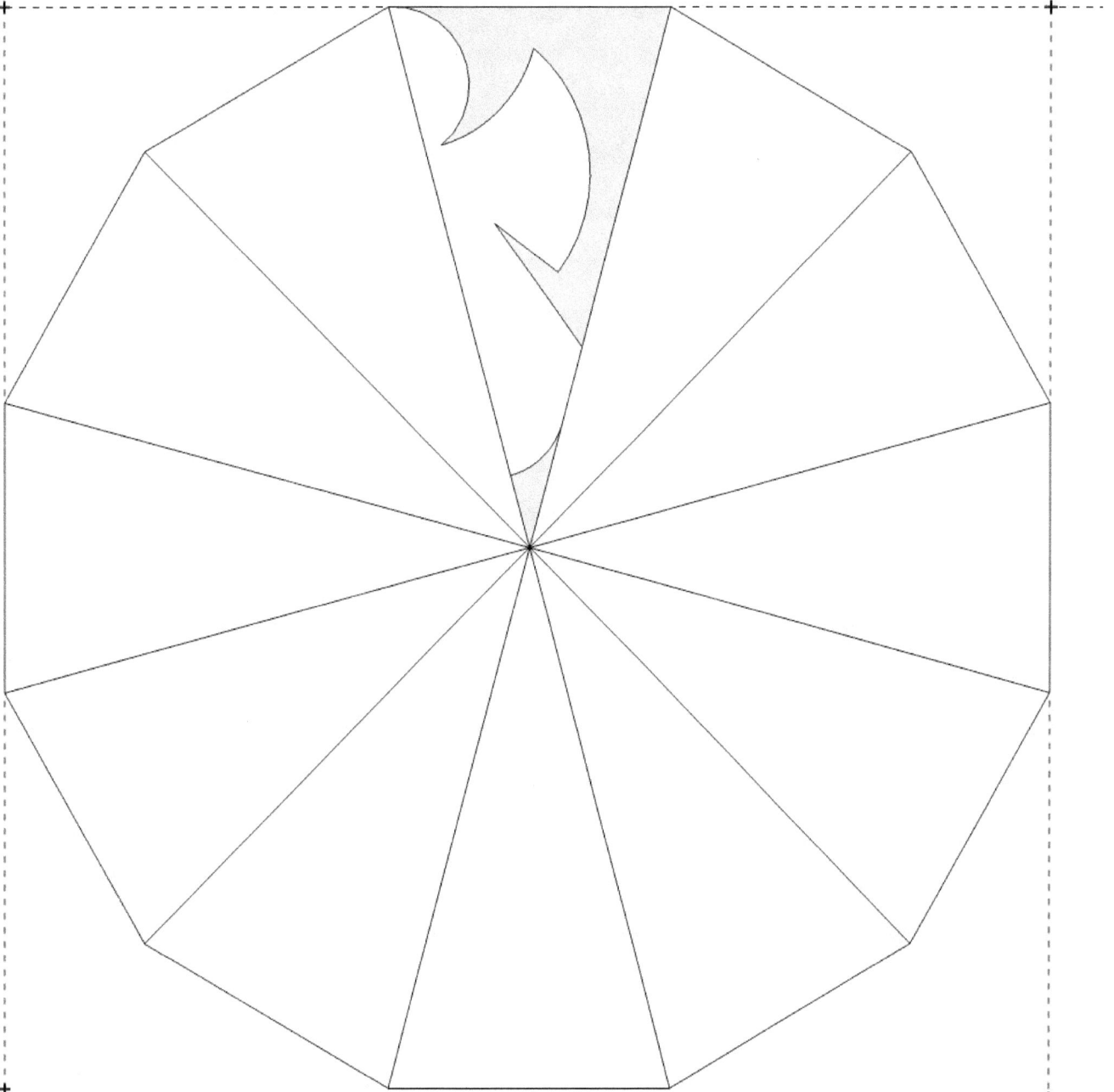

TRIANGLES AND CRESCENT

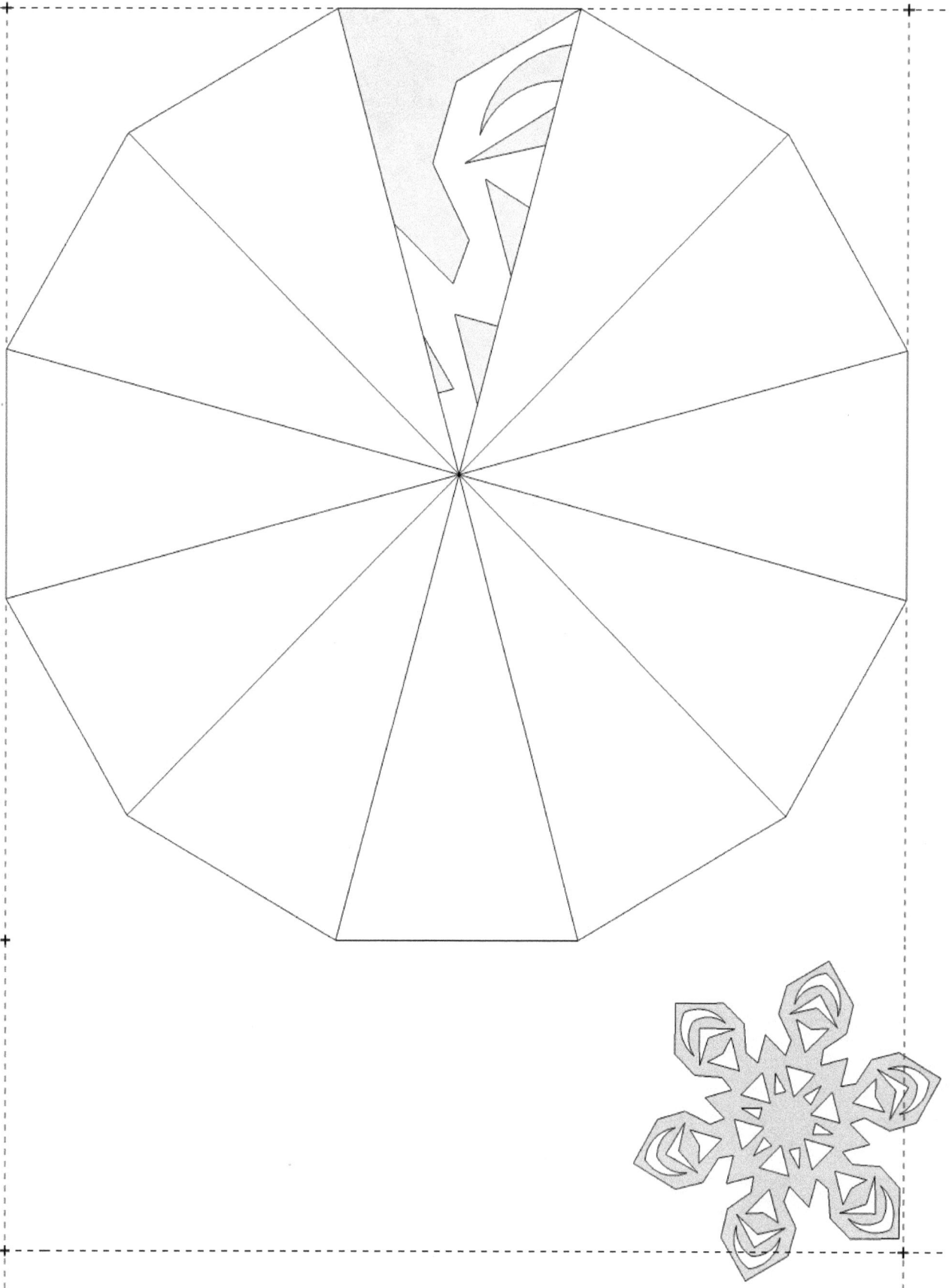

PINE TREE WITHIN PINE TREE

JOLLY BIRDS

THORNY

ROY YAP

PINE TREE CHEVRON

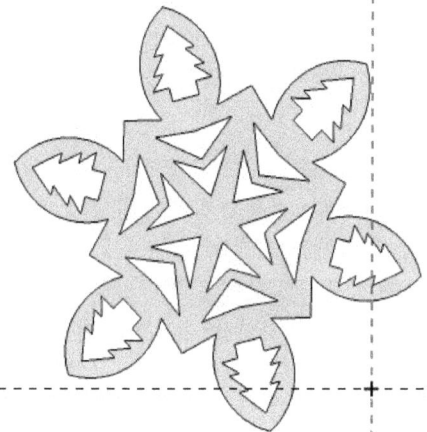

ICICLE

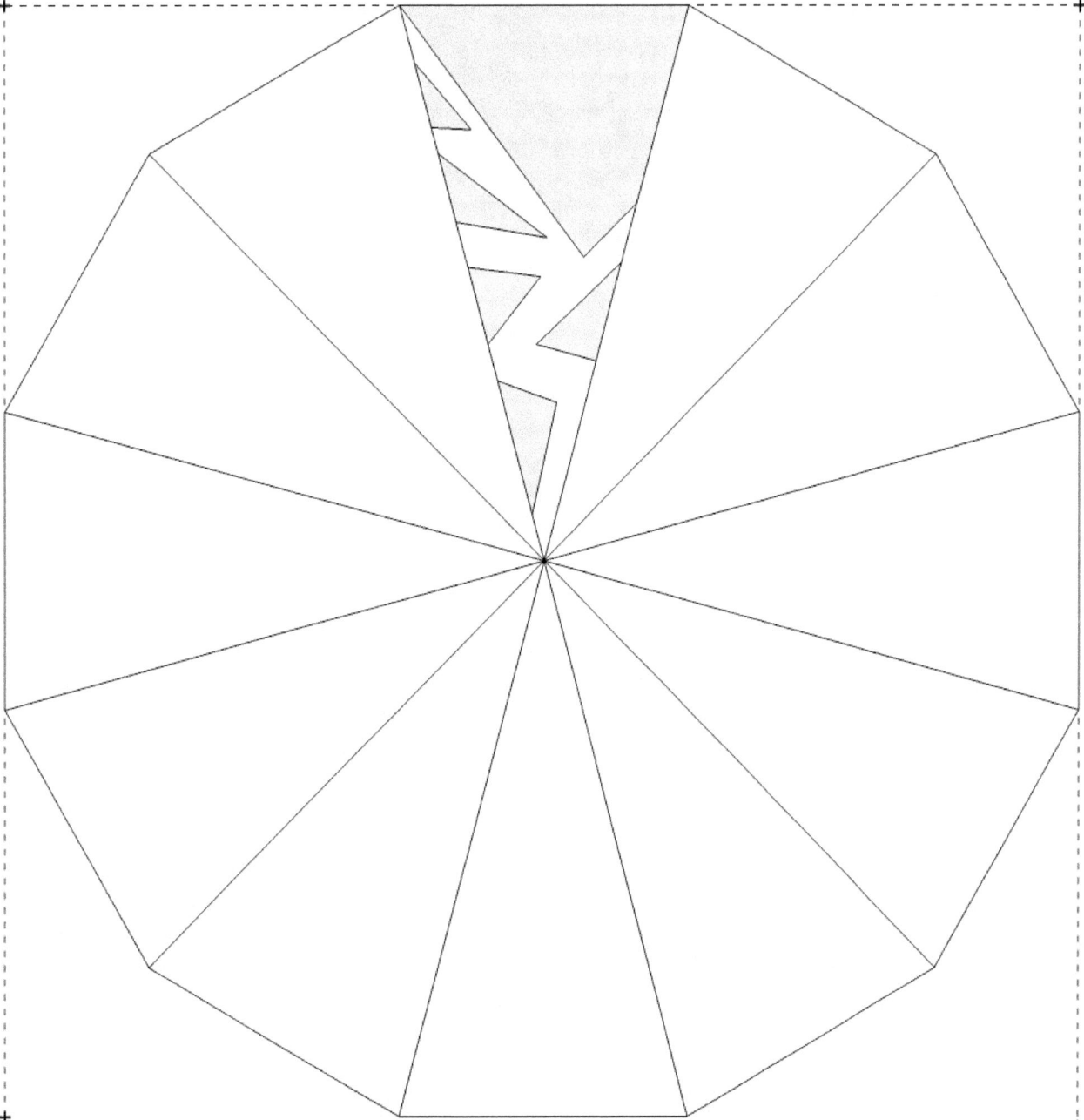

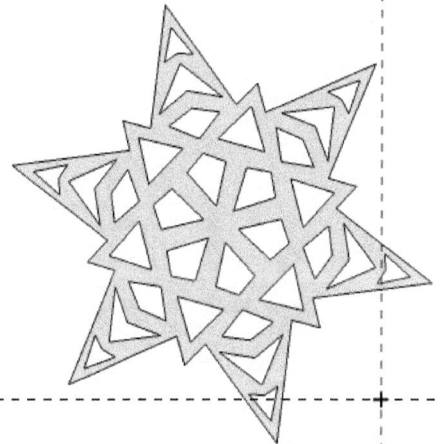

GIFT SNOWFLAKE

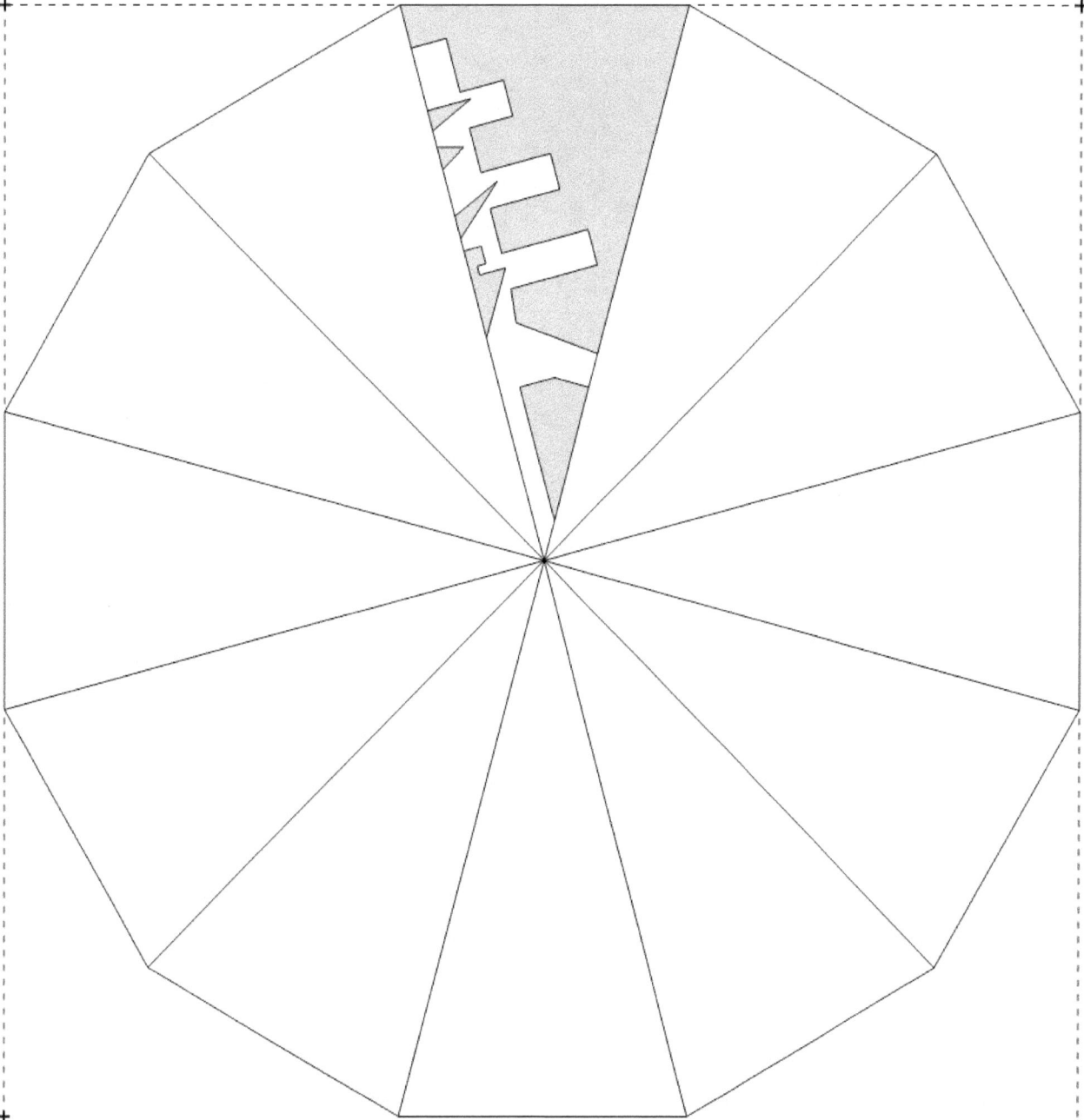

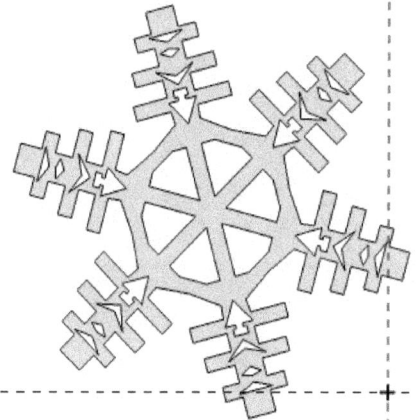

ROY YAP

SPACE NEEDLE

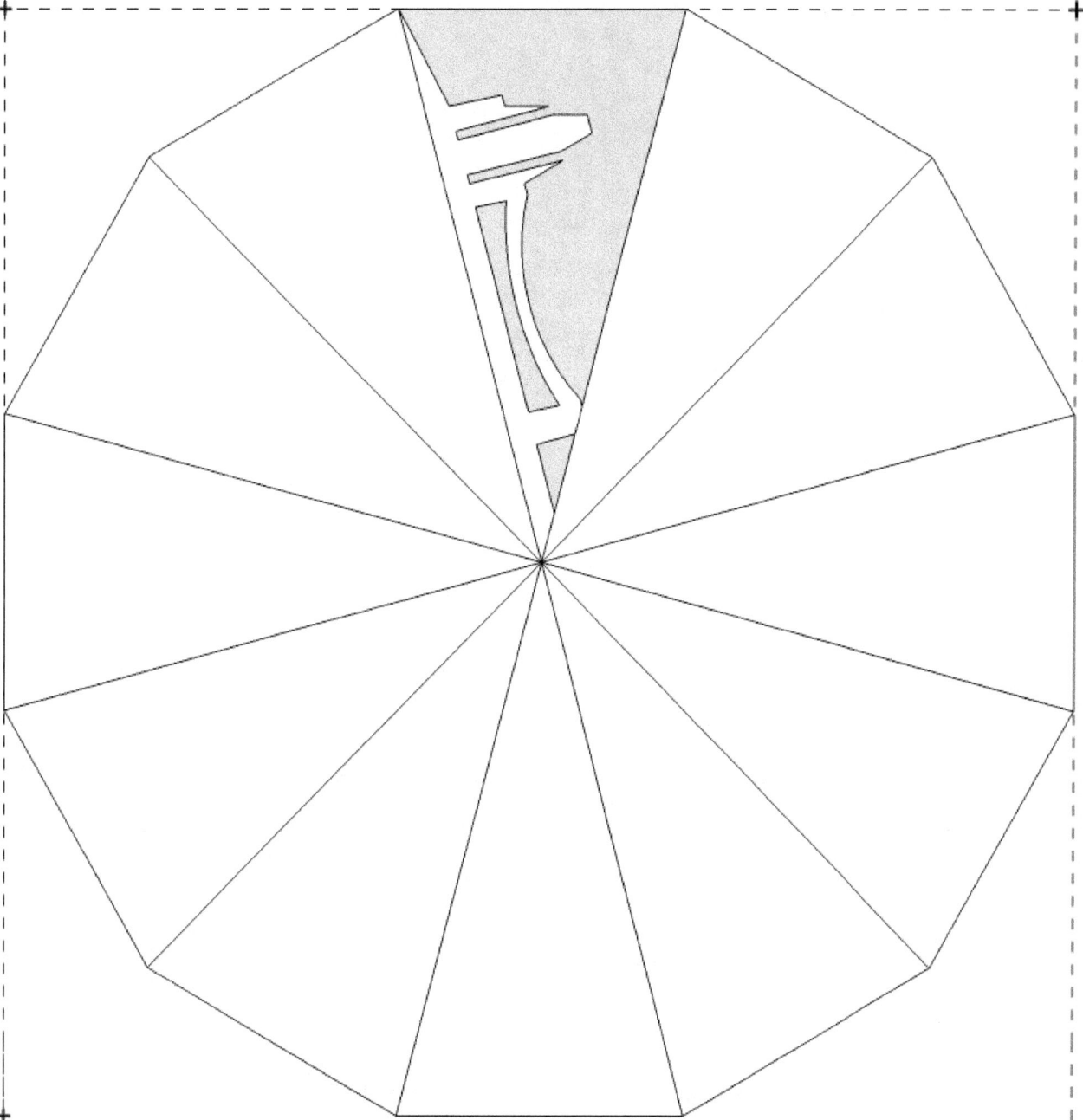

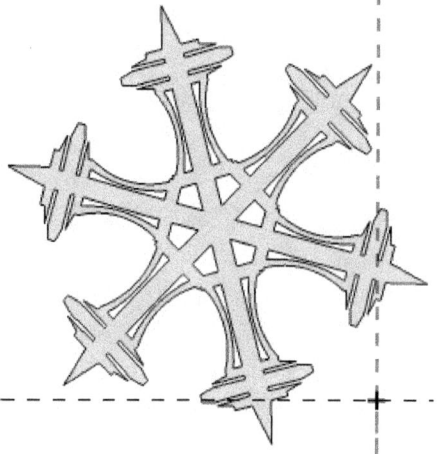

GUY AND GIRL

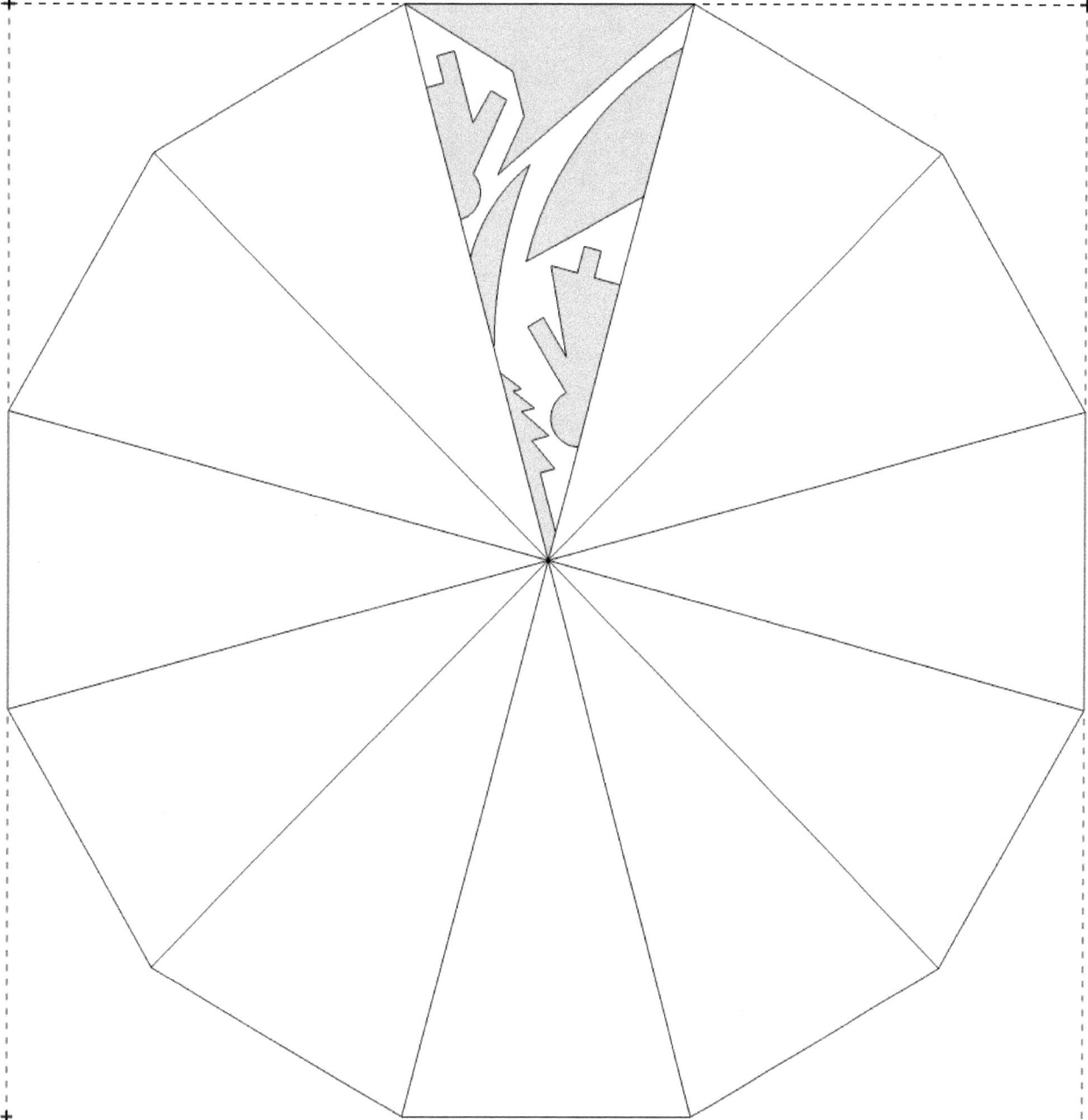

FLEUR-DE-LIS HEXAGON

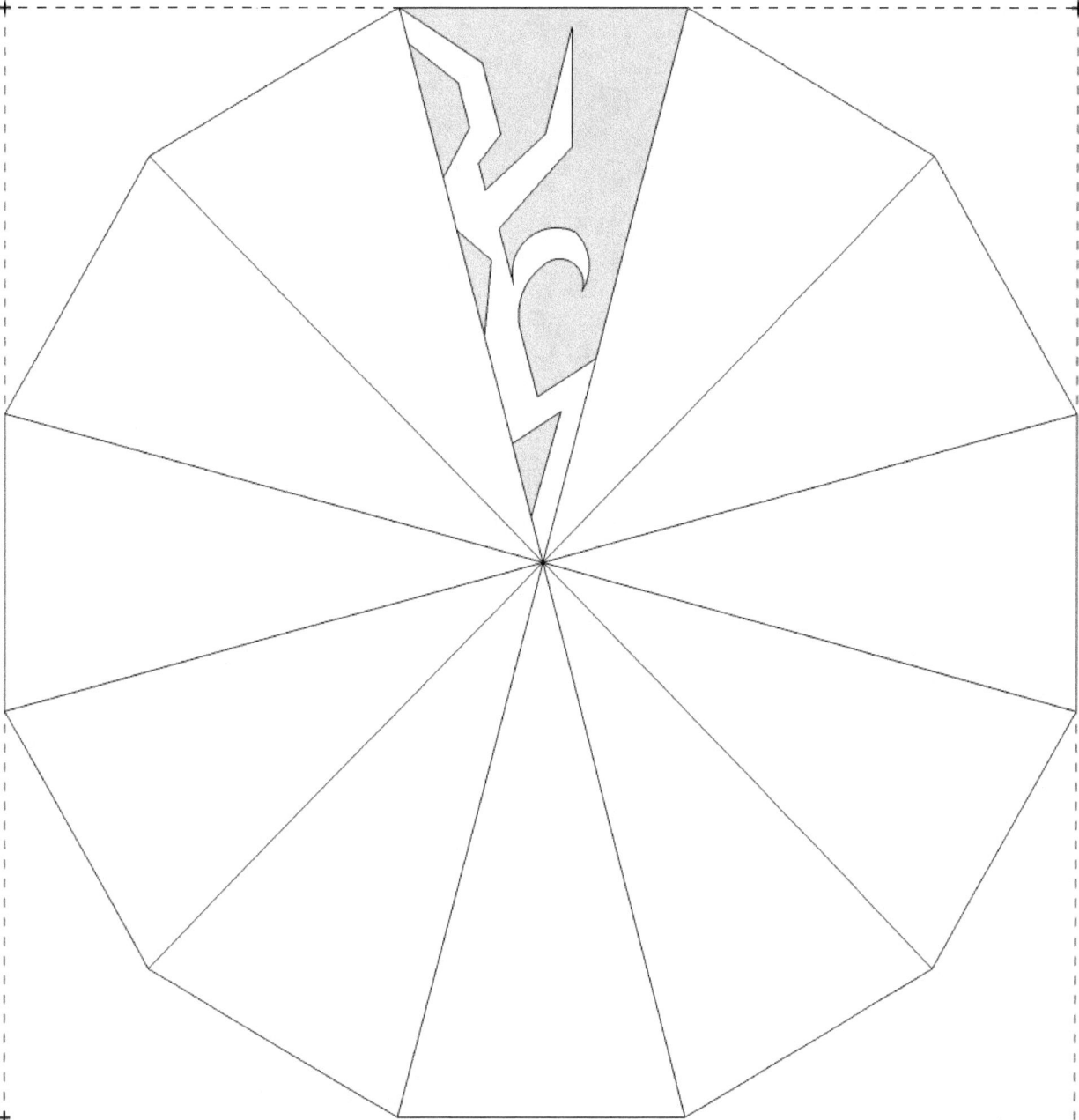

FUZZY

CAT

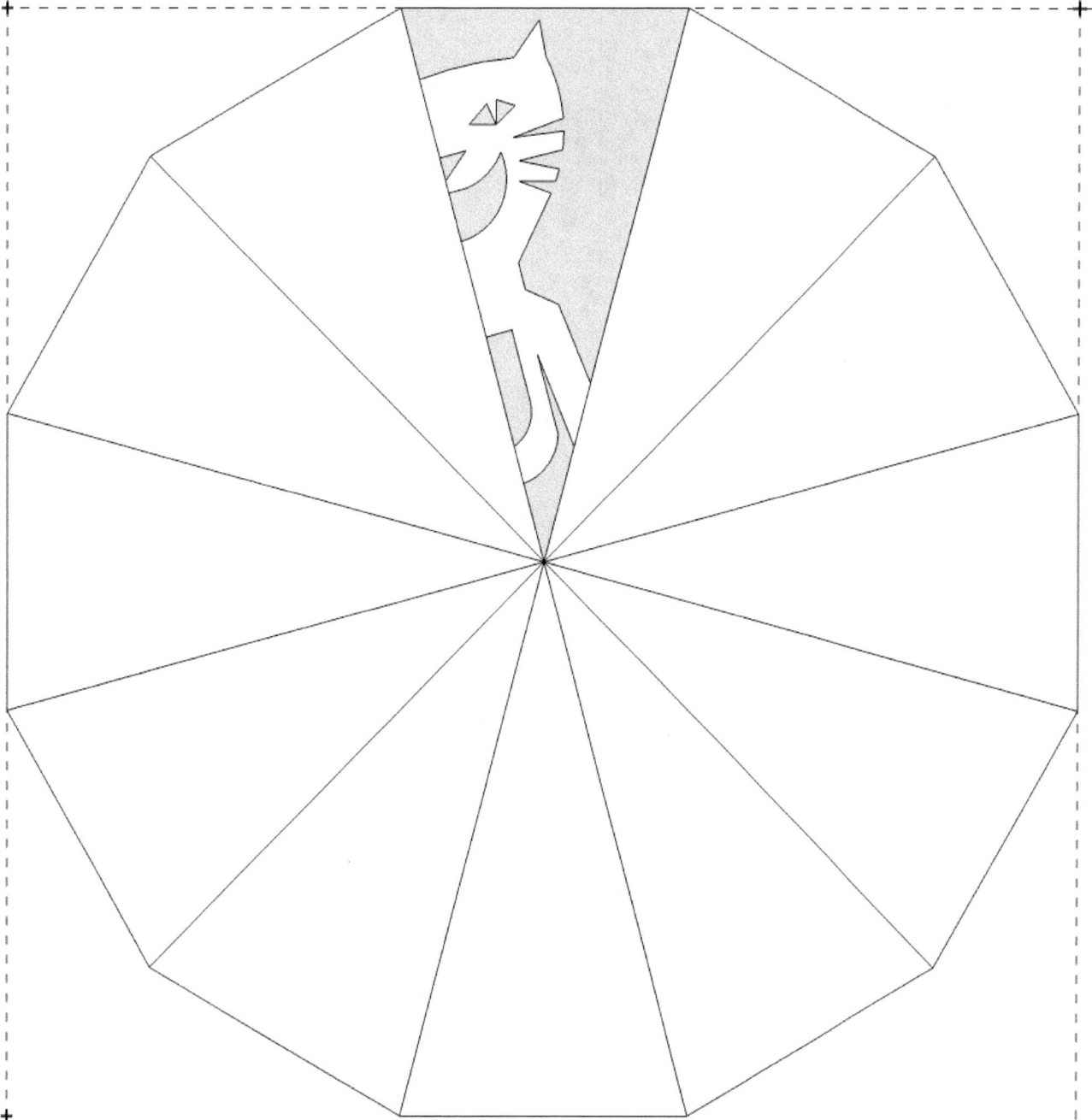

CHAINSAW

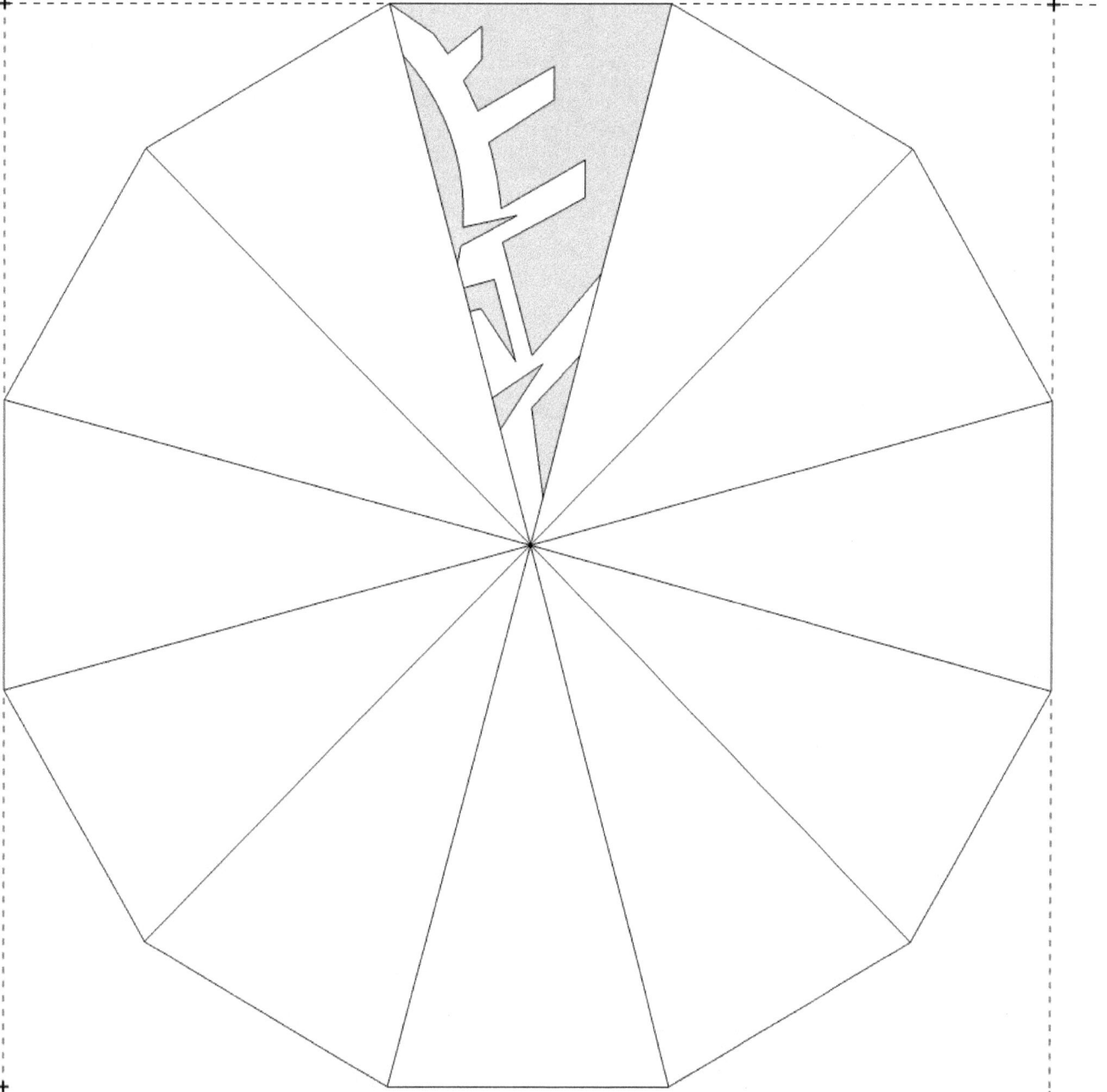

ULTIMATE SNOWFLAKE

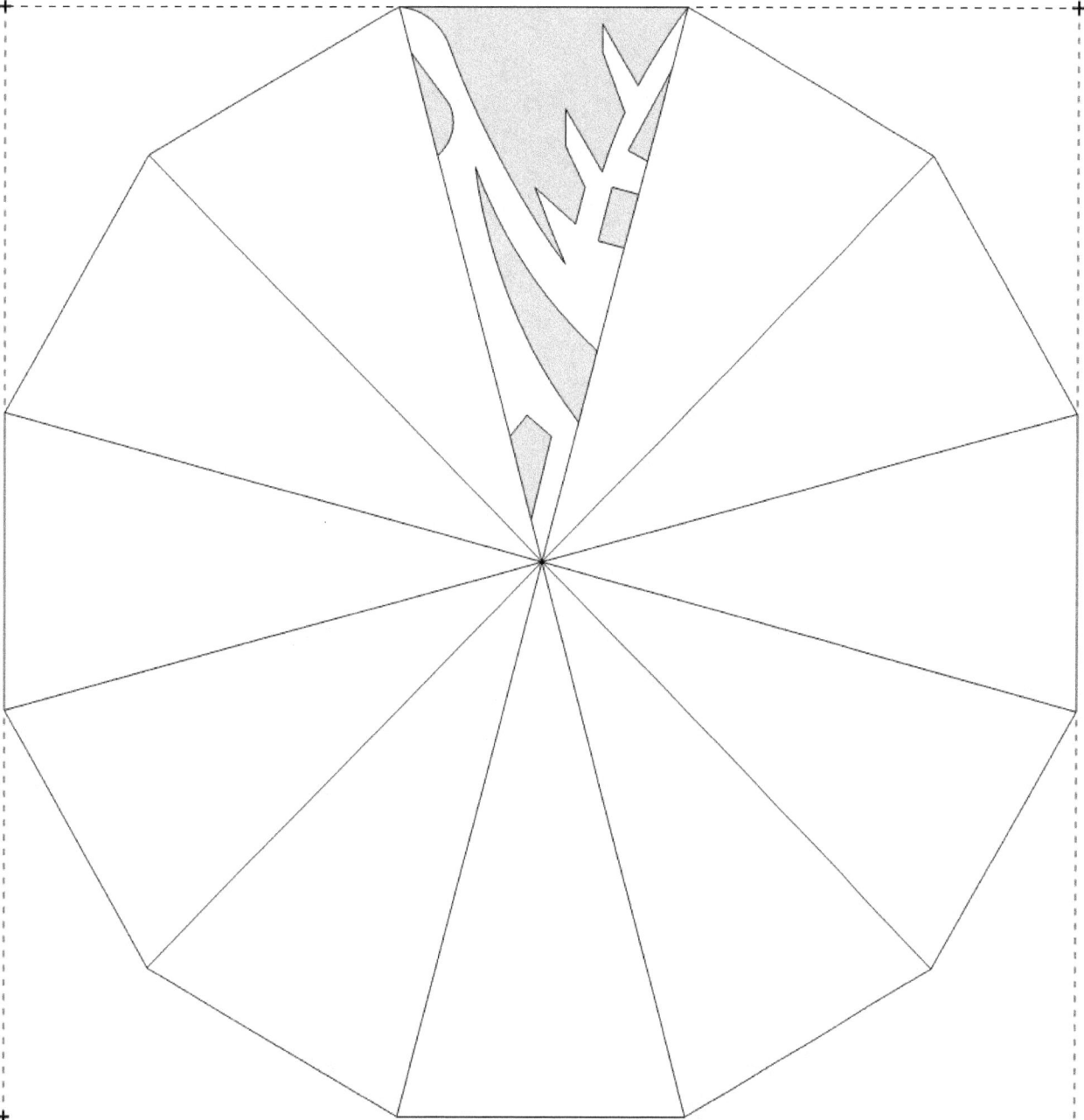

SNOW OWL

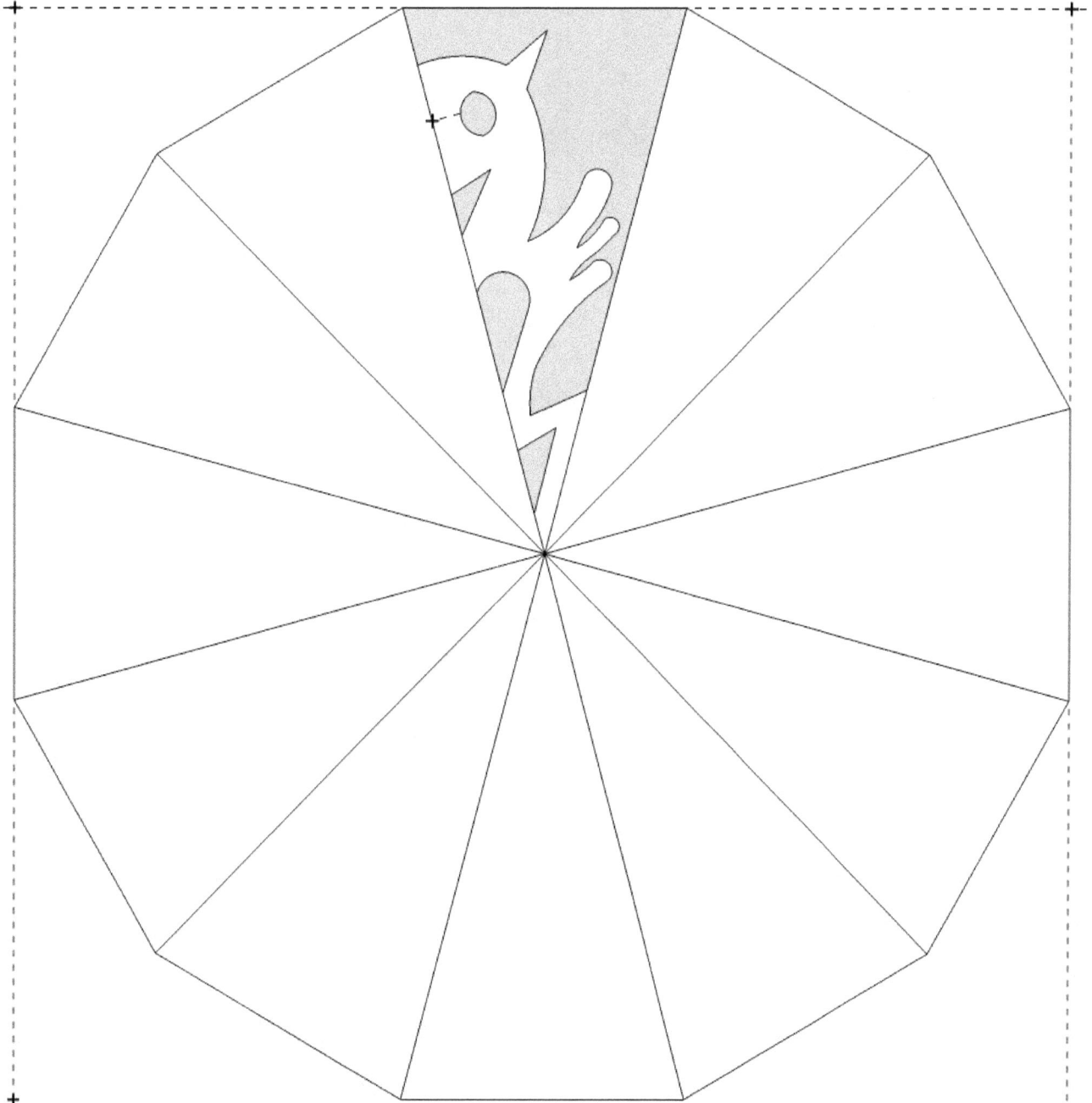

FOUR SIDED ANCHOR

THE BEE

ROCKET ASTRONAUT

PENGUINS

ARROWS

PUPPY AND PAWS

SNOWMAN AND REINDEER

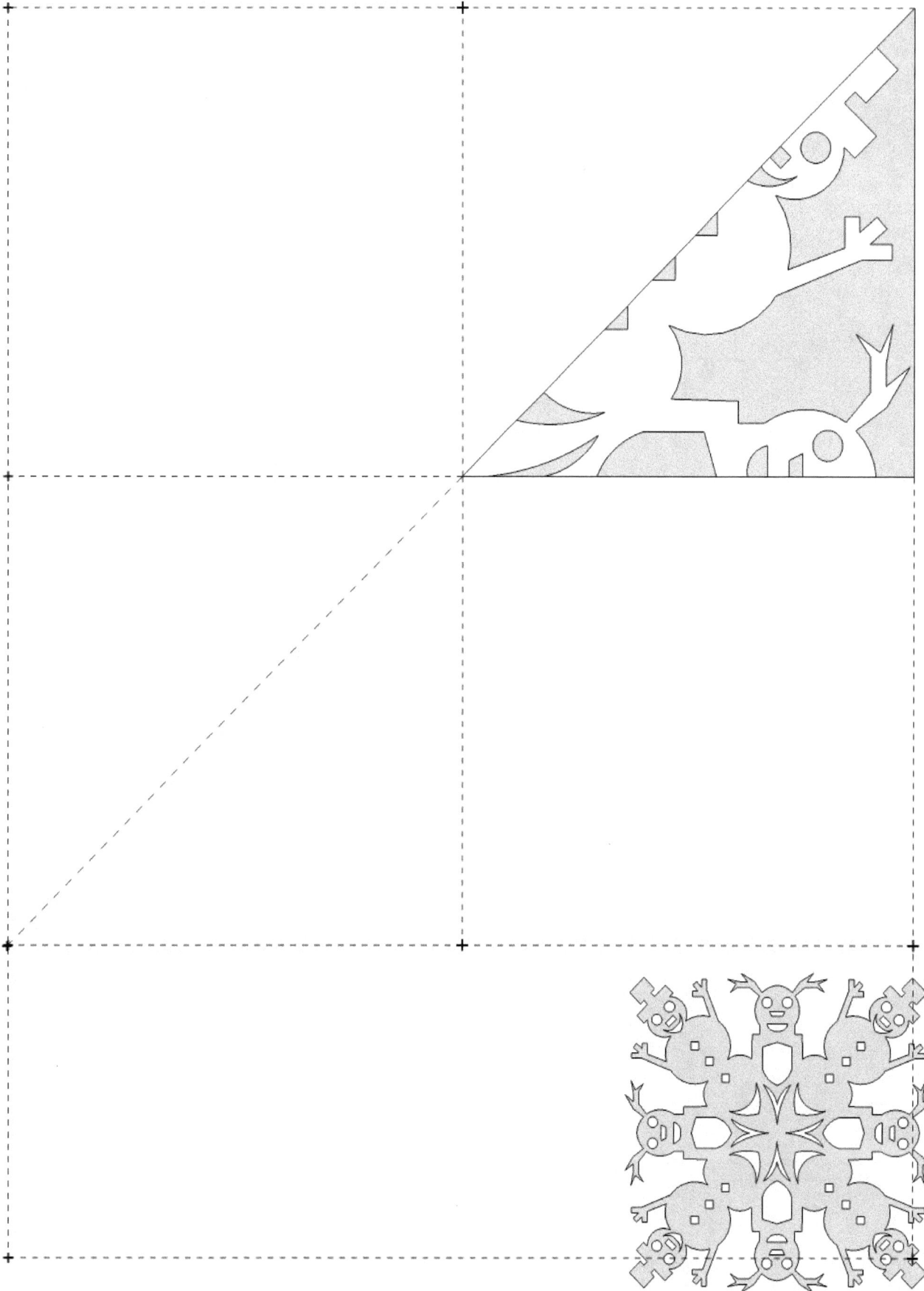

PINE TREE WITHIN PINE TREE

ABOUT THE AUTHOR

Roy Yap is a software test engineer by profession, a mechanical engineer by degrees and a tinkerer of technology. An eye for design, shapes and geometry, symmetry and a dash of experimental creativity is what drives his passion and ideas for snowflakes.

He is an avid bicyclist completing almost 5 double centuries since 2011. He currently lives in the great Pacific Northwest (Seattle, Washington) and is a "pet person", currently owned by a very cute male tuxedo cat named Desi.

https://royyap1.wixsite.com/worldofsnowflakes

https://www.facebook.com/WorldOfPaperSnowflakes

https://twitter.com/WorldSnowflakes

https://www.instagram.com/worldofpapersnowflakes/